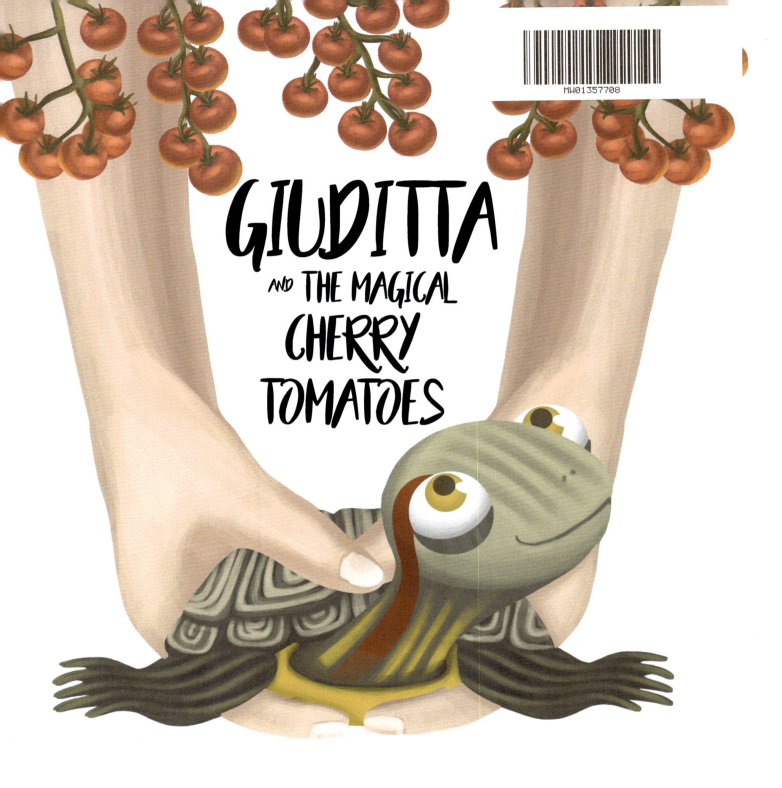

GIUDITTA
AND THE MAGICAL CHERRY TOMATOES

Natasha R.   Sofii O.

Natasha R.

All you need to know about me is that I really love nature and animals. I have always believed that I have a special connection to the animal kingdom. This belief has taken me on many adventures with different animals, "Giuditta" being just one of them. We shared a life for 11 years and during that time, I was able to observe an incredible number of signals that led me to believe this little turtle could feel and could reason, and she had intention and determination for sure. This is my first attempt at an illustrated children's story, and it would have never come to be without the lucky encounter with my co-author/illustrator Sophie O. I hope this is the first of many more stories we'll work on together, and I hope you enjoy it as much as we did while creating it.

Sofii O.

I love nothing more than drawing children's books about animals because the truth is that I am a big kid at heart. I am grateful for this collaboration with Natasha R. and for bringing to life the story of Giuditta. She made me believe that animals like Giuditta can feel, can be smart and have dreams. This little turtle is a source of inspiration and real wonder. I hope she will bring you a lot of positive emotions and make you smile. Let's start our adventure!

To Sky

"May the good memories always survive the storm"

It was an afternoon like many others for six-year-old Olly, but what he didn't know was that he was about to get his very first pet on that day. Little, green and oh-so-adorable, the creature was barely the size of a coin. It was a freshwater turtle—a red-eared slider terrapin to be exact—and it was going to be his job to take care of it. His mum said it was so he could learn a "sense of responsibility" or taking care of someone else who depends on you and can't really tell you much, just like a baby.

That cute little creature was many things, but it was certainly not fluffy, cuddly, or any of the things a pet should be. Olly could not even really play with it, as it was so delicate and really just meant to be left alone in the little oasis it came in.

"What should we call it?" he asked his mum.
"I don't know, I always liked the name Giuditta for a pet. Does this one look like a Giuditta?" she asked.
It sure did, and so its name was decided long before anyone even stopped to wonder if Giuditta was a male or a female turtle.

The first few weeks went by so fast. All day long, Giuditta would walk up to the top of the oasis then back down to the water. At the top, she would stretch and rest. At the bottom, she would swim and feed. Up and down, top to bottom, day after day.

She was an observer. When she was up top, she would look and stare and take in all the surroundings, but that was all she was doing. In no time, she became boring and irrelevant in the eyes of the young child. Mum ended up being tasked with keeping the little creature fed, clean and healthy, and that's how they bonded.

A year went by and Giuditta had grown. She had started to develop some interesting traits. She seemed to have come to fully understand the members of the family and her relationship with each of them. Mum was the provider of food. Whenever she passed in front of the little tank, Giuditta would move frantically in the water or tap the glass to get attention. As it turned out, this was her call for food and it quickly became their thing. Tap, food, agitate, food, swim and tap, food. She had quite an appetite for a small animal, preferring tiny dry shrimps to the traditional turtle nibbles.

She had also developed a love for music. Dad was an avid guitar player, so every time he took out his guitar, Giuditta would climb to the top and stretch her neck out as long as she could, sometimes her legs too. It was almost as if she was trying to fly. With her eyes closed, she appeared to be in her own little heaven. Mum always wondered what went on inside her little head. Did she have dreams of her own?

Nobody believed it until dad started to perform only for Giuditta. She would stare at him with eyes open in total adoration. She definitely loved the sound of his guitar and had a slight preference for rock and blues.

I think it's fair to say she was happy, and that happiness, food and music helped Giuditta grow and grow and grow and grow until she needed a bigger tank. The new tank was placed outside, under the porch. This meant that in the early hours of the day, before it was too hot, she could spend some time in the sun and allow her shell to dry. This was an essential part of her wellbeing as it stopped mold and other microbes from hatching on her.
It was a particularly hot summer's day. As usual, Giuditta was placed outside before the family went on with all their daily routines. Mum was running late that day; her chores had kept her away from the house for longer than expected and she reached home in the late afternoon.

She walked in, greeted the family, and was about to prepare dinner when her eyes stopped right where Giuditta should be. She should have been indoors on the table next to the sofa, but all she saw was an empty spot. Her heart sank. Giuditta was still outside. She had been outside all day, forgotten, under the scorching sun for hours and hours.
Mum took a sprint towards the porch and her jaw dropped in horror. There she was, her body half tilted to the side, immersed in the hot water with her eyes closed. She was shaking as if an electric current was running through her body.

"Help! Help! We need to save her!" mum shouted with tears running down her cheeks.

The veterinary clinic was already closed, so mum called the emergency number and a kind doctor explained what she should do.

"We need to lower her temperature, put her in cold water, and then monitor how she is doing. Make sure her head does not retreat inside the shell or she will likely die."

Mum had never been so desperate and full of guilt. She stayed up all night with her hands in the cold water, wrapped around Giuditta's body, massaging her legs, stretching her head out. Over and over again, she repeated how sorry she was and that she would not let her die—not today, not like this.

Giuditta survived the night, but she was not moving much. Clearly, she needed to rest and recover, but nobody knew how long that would take. Three days went by and mum decided to place her in the spare bathtub. It was big enough to allow her to swim and a safe upgrade from the outdoor tank, which helped relieve mum's immense sense of guilt for the accident that occurred.

The vet had told her to try to stimulate her with different foods, unusual foods, things she may find interesting and that could help revive her a little. Mum tried everything, all kinds of vegetables and even minced meat, as other terrapins' owners had suggested. But Giuditta just stayed there in the water, not moving, not opening her mouth at all.

As one last attempt, mum tried a ripe cherry tomato. It was so red, so ripe and so sweet. She placed it in the water and waved it in front of Giuditta who immediately came closer to get a better look, probably attracted by the bright colour. She slowly tried to open her mouth, but she had very little energy and could not bite on the tomato. Mum broke it into smaller pieces and slowly but surely, one piece at the time, Giuditta ate it all. And that's when the miracle happened.

Maybe it was a special tomato, or maybe mum had prayed so much that she made it happen, but almost as if she had been given a magic potion, Giuditta became more alert. She started swimming more, moving a lot, and became incredibly obsessed with cherry tomatoes. For days, she refused any other food but would gorge on tomatoes in frantic excitement.
Tomato is a fruit and, as such, it has sugars. Sugars are known for making our brains work, and Giuditta's brain started to work in ways nobody thought possible.

She became restless, like a person who just got a second chance at life. In fact, she did get just that, a second chance, and she had no intention of wasting it. There was a big, wide world to explore and little time to do it. But Giuditta's world was only as big as the second-floor spare bathtub. Bigger than her old tank, yet not quite a world.

On the third day of her recovery, and after much cherry tomato feasting, a strange thing happened. Mum walked into the bathroom to check on Giuditta and there she was, in an empty bathtub, with all the water gone and the plug moved to one side.
Mum called Olly to ask why he removed the water. The child denied doing any such thing, so mum got upset and grounded him for lying. It was only the two of them in the house, who else could have done it?

Mum refilled the bathtub and went on with her daily business. A few hours went by, but when she returned to check on Giuditta, the water was gone, and the plug was moved to one side again.
Mum thought that a practical joke was being played on her, so after some yelling at Olly, she decided to ignore the prank in the hopes that he would stop.

She filled the bathtub again and went to sleep. Just as she closed her eyes, she heard the distinctive sound of water going down the drain. Olly had been fast asleep for hours. She rushed to the bathroom and couldn't believe her eyes. There was Giuditta, floating in the whirlpool with her neck stretched out and looking straight into the drain, probably wondering "what's on the other side? How do I get there? Is this the way out to the world?" She was not swimming. Instead, she was caught in the whirlpool in a sort of suspended fantasy, spinning in a mix of awe and wonder. Mum could not believe her eyes. How did she even manage to take the plug out? What kind of reasoning is required to do that? Could it be that the sweet tomatoes and the heat stroke had made this turtle smarter? Nobody had an answer to this question, because nothing this odd had ever happened before.

This started a funny battle of the wits between mum and Giuditta. Mum tried in every way to prevent the turtle from taking the plug out. She piled all sorts of heavy weights like bricks, vases with plants on top of the plug, but Giuditta didn't give up. Even if it took an entire day of plotting, pushing and swimming against the weight, she always managed to unplug the bathtub. She wasn't just a smarter turtle, she was determined like no other. It seemed like she really wanted to go places. So, after a few days, partly won over by her determined character and partly because the water waste had become really significant, mum decided to let Giuditta roam freely around the house.
Imagine for a moment what that would be like. You have never been anywhere other than a small tank and then a bigger tank for years of your life, and now, finally, a world is opening up to you. Who wouldn't be excited?
Anyone who talks about the slow speed of a turtle has never met Giuditta! She could sprint from one side of the house to the other like a Hot Wheels toy car.

And then it happened again.
Mum started to hear a strange noise. It went like this: tunf...tunf...tunf....
What was it? Where was it coming from?
It sounded like something bouncing on the staircase. Wait, what?

She ran to the stairs looking for Giuditta, and there she found her. From the second floor, she had thrown herself down the steps, one by one. One tunf at a time, she had almost made it to the ground floor—clearly intending to go somewhere.
You see, there is one thing you need to know about the terrapins, once they decide on something, they will not give up until they get what they want.
Mum brought Giuditta upstairs again, but a few minutes later, the tunf, tunf, tunf began again. Giuditta was determined to explore the world downstairs too.

So, it was decided that day that Giuditta would live on the ground floor of the house. She immediately found a cosy place to hide during the day, crawling into a small opening under the kitchen cabinet.
In the morning, she would come out from her hiding place and wait in front of the fridge. She had quickly figured out that her favourite cherry tomatoes lived there.
Mum would put her in a plastic bowl filled with water and leave her inside until she was done with her food and had also gone to the toilet.
She would tap the bowl to let mum know when she wanted to come out, then off she went on her adventures around the house.

Giuditta could often be found hiding in the basket between the dog's plush toys, she loved to sleep on them, under them and anywhere in between.

Some days she just loved to crawl into the dog's bed and spread out like a starfish to make sure the dog knew who the boss was.
But most days, she would simply hide under the kitchen cabinet until she was hungry.

One day, she could not be found anywhere. The whole family looked and searched and looked and searched until they finally realised that the door to the porch had been left open for a while. Maybe Giuditta had seen the opportunity and made a quick escape? They searched around the garden, and just when they thought all hope had been lost, they spotted something moving in the pool. There she was, happily swimming laps in the water.
She saw mum approaching and quickly swam to the bottom of the pool, clearly not ready to come out yet.
Mum let her stay in a while longer. After all, a little chlorine never killed anyone!
Soon enough she got tired and swam to the top, making her way towards mum's hands and happy to be carried back inside the house.

This was just the first of many adventurous garden escapes.
One day, Giuditta was sucked into the pool filter on one of her garden adventures. The entire family panicked when she could not be found anywhere but were relieved to find that the filter had kept her safe and unharmed.
She was such a smart turtle that the next time she jumped into the pool, she figured out a way to anchor herself to the edge of the filter opening, which allowed her to take advantage of the current to just float and nap at the same time.

Another day, after spending a lot of time in the garden—though the family had not even realised she was gone—she decided to come back inside by herself. When she discovered that the glass door was now closed, she cleverly tapped with her long claws to get someone's attention.
Tap, tap, tap. As soon as the door opened, she walked in without a care in the world and went straight to the fridge demanding ripe tomatoes for dinner.

Over time, her claws grew so long that they were kind of scary. Mum searched for information online about why Giuditta's claws had grown so much, but what she discovered left her speechless.
It appeared that Giuditta was in fact a male turtle! However, the family had grown so fond of that name and were so accustomed to referring to it as "she" that they decided to disregard this new piece of evidence and continued calling him Giuditta.

It was the beginning of fall when Giuditta discovered the world around the corner. She literally walked the perimeter of the house all the way to the front, all the way to the main gate, and then all the way to an opening high enough to allow a quick escape onto the road.
She was a mere meter away from the gate, rushing fast towards the other side, towards the world she wondered about. Luckily, mum saw her just in time and grabbed her just before she made it through and brought her back inside.

She was returned safely back to the house— and back to her daily routine of plush toys, tomatoes and hide and seek games with the family— but it was clear that after discovering the world beyond the corner, there was no going back to normal life for her.

Giuditta's mind was set on the next phase: conquering the world beyond the corner, on the other side of the gate. It was the call of the unknown, and it became her only reason for waking up every day and eating so many tomatoes. She needed to have enough energy to attempt another escape.
It would be only a matter of time before someone forgot to close that door again, and Giuditta would be right there, ready to take her chance.

It was a late winter afternoon. Even for a hot place like Dubai, the temperature was getting cooler and it was dark already. Mum was calling and searching everywhere when it became clear that it had indeed finally happened. Nobody was able to recall opening the door or leaving it open at all, but Giuditta was gone — gone for good.

Searching the streets did not help, placing ads in the lost and found pets of the neighbourhood did not help. Determined and adventurous Giuditta was finally gone and was never coming back.

It had been 11 years since the day Giuditta came home from the pet shop, and now she was out there in the world exploring it the way she clearly always dreamt of. Everyone hopes that she is still out there, maybe with another family, trying hard to escape another garden. After all, terrapins can live for up to 40 years and she had a lot of life left to live. Terrapins are no ordinary pets, and Giuditta was definitely extraordinary, the smartest of them all!

> Wherever you may be, little turtle explorer, we hope you think of us when you hear the sound of a guitar, eat a ripe cherry tomato, or just float in your world of fantasy.
>
> We have learned a lot from you. Thank you for our time together and for showing us that even the smallest heart holds desires, and it is only fair to fulfil a heart's dream when a new chance is given. May we all be more like you and live with the same determination and curiosity.

Never has anyone been so curious and determined to see the world as Giuditta, the red-eared slider.

THE END

"This book is printed in the Dyslexie Font a typeface designed for people with dyslexia. For more information go to www.dyslexiefont.com"

Made in the USA
Columbia, SC
22 February 2019